Hello
KNITTING!

Hello

KNITTING!

Simple knits to have you in stitches

PAVILION

First published in the United
Kingdom in 2015 by
Pavilion Books Company Limited
1 Gower Street
London
WC1E 6HD

Copyright © Pavilion Books 2015

ISBN 978-1-909815-96-4

A CIP catalogue record for this
book is available from the British
Library.

10 9 8 7 6 5 4 3 2 1

Reproduction by Mission,
Hong Kong
Printed and bound by 1010
Printing International Ltd, China

This book can be ordered direct
from the publisher at
www.pavilionbooks.com

Contents

Introduction

In this book we aim to introduce you to the versatility of the craft of knitting. Whether you are a relative beginner or an experienced crafter looking to broaden your range of skills, you should be able to find a project here that will inspire you to take up your needles and cast on.

The projects include some small-scale, simple pieces that are quick to make, such as the elegant Beaded jewellery (page 38) and the quirky Animal ears (page 32). We then progress to more complex and larger items that require more investment of time and skill to produce, such as the Toddler's sweater (page 73) – a great introduction to garment knitting if you haven't tried this before – and the Textured cushion (page 104), which incorporates a number of different techniques to gorgeous effect.

We have also tried to offer a variety of projects that will fulfil different purposes, whether you want to make some stylish accessories for yourself, knit some bootees to keep a special baby's feet warm or make an eye-catching piece of décor for your home.

Techniques

This book features a wide variety of inspiring techniques for you to master. In this section we review the basics, such as casting on, casting off and making the main stitches, and then go on to introduce more advanced skills such as cables and colourwork.

Starting Off

In this book we've gathered together projects that are fun and inspiring and that will introduce you to a variety of versatile techniques. Before you start stitching, here are a few things to consider.

Yarns

Each project specifies what sort of yarn you need to complete the item. Often you will be able to substitute the yarn for one that you already have or would prefer to use. Just bear in mind what the purpose of the project is. For a garment or accessory such as the Toddler's sweater (page 73), the Baby bootees (page 56) or the Cable legwarmers (page 46), you will want to use a yarn that is soft and comfortable to wear against the skin, is easy to launder and is somewhat stretchy and pliable. For projects that are primarily decorative – the Lucky cat (page 80), the Doorstop (page 92) or the Finger puppets (page 62) – you could use an economical yarn such as a synthetic fibre, and be bold and experimental with the colour choices.

Materials

Your main equipment will, of course, be your knitting needles. Most of the projects in this book use standard straight needles, but some of them require you to knit in the round using double-pointed needles or a circular needle. You will also need a cable needle (a double-pointed needle with a kink in it) to make the Cable legwarmers (page 46) and the Table runner (page 98).

Other useful tools are a tapestry needle (a blunt, large-eyed needle) to weave in ends and join seams; a measuring tape to check the size of work in progress; and scissors to cut the yarn. Any other specific tools or materials that are required are listed at the start of each project.

Basic Techniques

Whether you are a beginner seeking guidance or an experienced crafter in need of a reminder, in this section we set out the basic techniques you will need to start tackling the projects in this book.

Slip knot

The very beginning – getting your first loop of yarn onto the needle!

1 Wind the yarn around two fingers twice.

2 Insert a knitting needle through the first (front) strand and under the second (back) one.

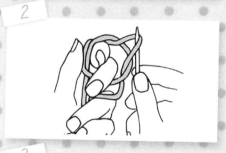

3 Pull the back strand through the front one to form a loop. Holding the loose ends of the yarn with your left hand, pull the needle upwards to tighten the knot. Pull the ball end of the yarn again to tighten the knot further.

Casting on

There are many possible ways to cast on (that is, to get the required number of stitches on the needle to be able to start knitting the first row); here and overleaf we explain two commonly used methods.

Thumb method

1 Make a slip knot 100cm (40in) from the end of the yarn. Hold the needle in your right hand with the ball end of the yarn over your index finger. *Wind the loose end of the yarn around your left thumb from front to back.

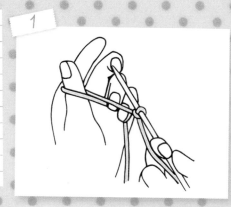

2 Insert the point of the needle under the first strand of yarn on your thumb.

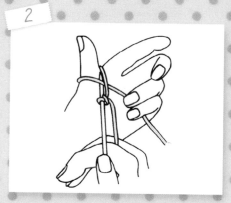

3 With your right index finger, take the ball end of the yarn over the point of the needle.

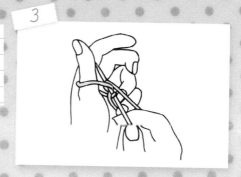

4 Pull a loop through to form the first stitch. Remove your left thumb from the yarn.

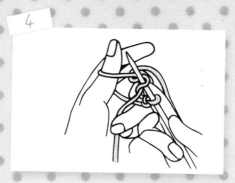

5 Pull the loose end to secure the stitch. Repeat from * until the required number of stitches have been cast on.

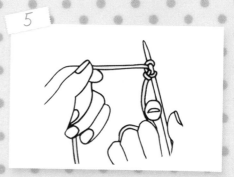

Cable method

1 This method of casting on requires two needles. Make a slip knot about 10cm (4in) from the end of the yarn. Hold this needle in your left hand.

2 Insert the right-hand needle through the slip knot. Wrap the yarn over the point of the right-hand needle.

3 Pull a loop through the slip knot with the right-hand needle.

4 Place this loop on the left-hand needle. Gently pull the yarn to secure the stitch.

5 Insert the right-hand needle between the slip knot and the first stitch on the left-hand needle. Wrap the yarn around the point of the right-hand needle.

6 Draw a loop through and place this loop on the left-hand needle. Repeat steps 5 and 6 until the required number of stitches have been cast on.

The knit stitch

1 Hold the needle with the cast-on stitches in your left hand, with the loose yarn at the back of the work. Insert the right-hand needle from left to right through the front of the first stitch on the left-hand needle.

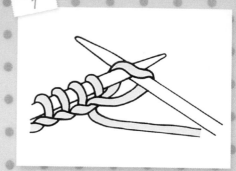

2 Wrap the yarn from left to right over the point of the right-hand needle.

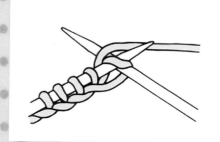

3 Draw the yarn through the stitch, thus forming a new stitch on the right-hand needle.

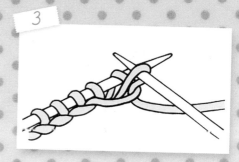

4 Slip the original stitch off the left-hand needle, keeping the new stitch on the right-hand needle.

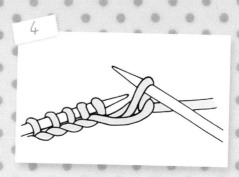

5 To knit a row, repeat steps 1 to 4 until all the stitches have been transferred from the left-hand needle to the right-hand needle. Turn the work, transferring the needle with the stitches to your left hand to work the next row.

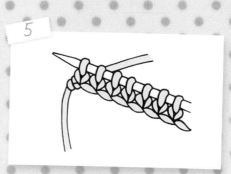

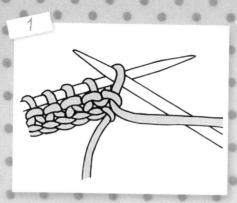

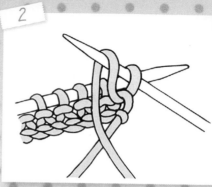

The purl stitch

1 Hold the needle with the stitches in your left hand, with the loose yarn at the front of the work. Insert the right-hand needle from right to left into the front of the first stitch on the left-hand needle.

2 Wrap the yarn from right to left, up and over the point of the right-hand needle.

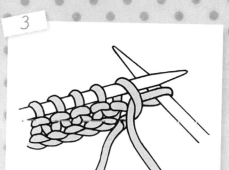

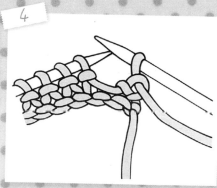

3 Draw the yarn through the stitch, thus forming a new stitch on the right-hand needle.

4 Slip the original stitch off the left-hand needle, keeping the new stitch on the right-hand needle.

5 To purl a row, repeat steps 1 to 4 until all the stitches have been transferred from the left-hand needle to the right-hand needle. Turn the work, transferring the needle with the stitches to your left hand to work the next row.

Casting off

This is the most common method of securing stitches after finishing a piece of knitting (known in the US as binding off). The cast-off edge should have the same elasticity as the knitted fabric, and you should cast off in the stitch used for the main fabric unless the pattern directs otherwise.

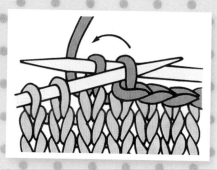

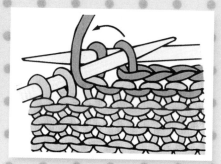

Casting off knitwise

Knit two stitches. *Using the point of the left-hand needle, lift the first stitch on the right-hand needle over the second and drop it off the needle. Knit the next stitch. Repeat from * until all the stitches have been worked off the left-hand needle and only one stitch remains on the right-hand needle. Cut the yarn, leaving enough to sew in the end, thread the end through the stitch and slip it off the needle. Draw the yarn up firmly to fasten off.

Casting off purlwise

Purl two stitches. *Using the point of the left-hand needle, lift the first stitch on the right-hand needle over the second and drop it off the needle. Purl the next stitch. Repeat from * until all the stitches have been worked off the left-hand needle and only one stitch remains on the right-hand needle. Secure the last stitch as described in casting off knitwise.

Knitted fabric

Combining knit and purl stitches in different ways produces different types of knitted fabric.

Stocking stitch

Stocking stitch fabric (known in the US as stockinette) is the standard knitted fabric, created by alternating knit and purl rows. The knit side is usually the 'right' side and the purl side the 'wrong' side. In this book, the Fair Isle tote and beret (page 48) are worked in stocking stitch. Working stocking stitch so the purl side is the right side creates reverse stocking stitch; this is used for the Hot water bottle cover (page 88).

Garter stitch

Garter stitch fabric is created by knitting every row. This creates quite a dense and bumpy-looking fabric that will be somewhat thicker than stocking stitch fabric. The Toddler's sweater (page 73) and the Contrast-edge slippers (page 56) are made in garter stitch.

Moss stitch

Moss stitch fabric (known in the US as seed stitch) is made by alternating knit and purl stitches within a row (k1, p1). On the reverse side, you need to make sure you purl the knit stitches from the previous row, and knit the purl stitches; if you knit the knits and purl the purls you will created ribbing instead. Moss stitch creates quite a bumpy-looking, textured fabric. Moss stitch is featured on the Textured cushion (page 104) and the Textured shoes (page 59).

Ribbing

Ribbing is made by alternating knit and purl stitches within a row – often k2, p2, but other combinations can be used. On the reverse side, you knit the knit stitches and purl the purl stitches from the previous row to maintain the pattern. Ribbing creates a characteristic corrugated effect, often seen on the cuffs and hems of knitwear. The tops and bottoms of the Cable legwarmers (page 46) are worked in a k1, p1 rib stitch.

Further Skills

Once you know the basics you will want to push your skills further. This book features a wide range of techniques that will expand your knitting vocabulary and enable you to make some innovative and stylish pieces.

Increasing

This book features several methods of increasing:

Kfb/pfb/inc: Knit or purl into the front and then the back of the same stitch to increase by one stitch.

M1: Pick up the strand of yarn lying between the next two stitches, put it on the left needle and knit it (or purl if appropriate) to make one stitch.

Decreasing

This book features several methods of decreasing:

K2tog: Insert the right-hand needle knitwise into the second stitch from the tip of the left-hand needle and through the next stitch on the left-hand needle. Pull the yarn through the two loops to make the new knit stitch.

P2tog: Insert the right-hand needle purlwise into the first two stitches on the left-hand needle and purl them together to make the new stitch. K3tog and p3tog decreases can be worked in a similar way.

Skpo: Slip the first stitch, knit the next stitch, pass the slipped stitch over (similar to casting off).

Sppo: Slip the first stitch, purl the next stitch, pass the slipped stitch over.

Ssk: Slip the first stitch knitwise, slip the second stitch in the same way, then knit the two stitches together through the front loops.

Cables

Cables, with their distinctive interlocking patterns, feature in the Cable legwarmers (page 46) and the Table runner (page 98). Cables can look complex but are in fact quite simple to make. You will need a cable needle, which looks like a short double-pointed needle with a kink in it to hold stitches. Otherwise, you can use a standard double-pointed needle. Knit to the point in the pattern where you need to make a cable. Slip the stated number of stitches (usually 2, 3 or 4) onto the cable needle and hold it at the back or front of the work as directed. Knit or purl the next stitches from the left-hand needle as instructed, and then knit or purl the stitches from the cable needle. The stitches will appear twisted, and this twist will eventually resolve into the cable pattern.

Lace

Lace knitting can be very complex and intricate, but in this book we feature only one simple lace project, the Lacy shawl (page 70). The main feature of lace knitting is pairing together increases and decreases to create the 'holes' of the lace. The Lacy shawl pattern pairs together an m1 increase with a k2tog decrease.

Eyelets and buttonholes

A similar method is used to make eyelets, such as those created for the drawstring of the Fair Isle tote (page 48), and buttonholes, such as those on the Textured cushion (page 104).

You cast off a certain number of stitches on the row where the eyelets or buttonholes are to be set; then on the next row you cast on over the cast-off stitches.

I-cord

I-cord is a length of knitted cord. This is used in the Animal ears (page 32), the Beaded jewellery (page 38), for the handle of the Doorstop (page 92) and for the Lucky cat's collar (page 80). You will need two short double-pointed needles. The stitches always remain on one of the needles, while you knit with the other. Cast on the desired number of stitches (usually between 2 and 5) to one needle. Knit those stitches as usual, but instead of turning the work, push the stitches to the other end of the needle. The working end of the yarn will be on the left-hand side instead of the usual right-hand side. Pull the working end across the back of the work, and knit the stitches again; try to knit the first stitch fairly tightly. Continue in this way, pushing the worked stitches to the other end of the needle and knitting them again, until the cord is the desired length.

Colourwork

The projects in this book feature the two main methods of colourwork: intarsia and Fair Isle.

Intarsia

The intarsia technique is generally used for discrete blocks of colour within a pattern. This method is used to make the darker-coloured cable section in the Table runner (page 98) and is featured in the Animal ears (page 32), where the inner part of the front of the ear is a different colour from the outer part.

You will need to wind a small bobbin of each colour used within the row (this makes the colour changes easier to work and means you are less likely to tangle up the different strands of yarn). For the Animal ears, for example, you will need one bobbin for the first MC section, a second bobbin for the CC section and a third bobbin for the second MC section. At the points where you change colours, you will need to twist the different yarns together at the

back of the work or you will be left with gaps in the knitted fabric. There will also be more yarn ends to weave in when you have finished!

Fair Isle

Fair Isle patterns have a very long history in knitting. These are intricate and small-scale patterns usually featuring two colours in a single row. The two colour yarns are 'stranded'; that is, the colour yarn that is not in use is left at the back of the work until needed. The loops formed by this are called 'floats'; it is important that they are not pulled too tightly when you are working the next stitch in that colour, as that will pucker the knitted fabric.

Fair Isle patterns are generally worked from a chart so that it is easy to follow the colour changes. Fair Isle patterns are featured on the Fair Isle tote and beret (page 48) and the Textured cushion (page 104).

Working from Patterns

Here are a few hints on working from patterns, including the importance of tension and an explanation of the abbreviations used in the pattern instructions in this book.

Materials

This section lists the materials required to complete the project, including the amount and colours of yarn, sizes of needles and any extras such as buttons or lining fabric.

Size

We give the finished size of each project so you know what to aim for. Tension is not essential for every project, but where tension details are listed you will need to achieve the correct tension in order to end up with the finished piece at the intended size.

Tension

Tension (known in the US as gauge) can differ quite significantly between knitters because of the way that the needles and yarn are held. It is particularly important to check your tension with the projects in this book as we give quite generic descriptions of the yarn required. To work a tension swatch, use the same needles, yarn and stitch pattern as those that will be used for the main work and knit a sample at least 12.5cm (5in) square. Smooth out the finished piece on a flat surface, but do not stretch it.

To check the stitch tension, place a ruler horizontally on the sample, measure 10cm (4in) across and mark with a pin at each end. Count the number of stitches between the pins.

To check the row tension, place a ruler vertically on the sample, measure 10cm (4in) and mark with pins. Count the number of rows between the pins.

If you have more stitches and rows than specified in the pattern, your tension is too tight; try again, using larger needles.

If you have fewer stitches and rows than specified, your tension is too loose; try again, using smaller needles.

Making up/Finishing

This section provides instructions on how to join the knitted pieces together, if relevant, and how to add any finishing touches, such as sewing in linings, adding buttons or embroidering details.

Sewing up seams

You can use ordinary backstitch to sew up some seams. This is the most suitable stitch, for example, if you are sewing a circular base into a bag, or sewing two different-shaped edges together.

If you are sewing a straight seam, then mattress stitch works well. Lay the pieces right side up and next to each other. You work up the side of the knitted pieces between the edge stitch and the next stitch – the edge stitch from each side will disappear into the seam. Insert the tapestry needle between the edge and next stitch on one knitted piece and thread it up the column between those two stitches, going under two stitch bars. Move over to the other piece and do the same. Go back to the point where the needle came out on the first piece and put it back in, going up the column under the next two bars. Continue going back and forth, pulling the thread tight each time. You will see that the two edges are pulled together.

Weaving in ends

Once your project has been sewn together, the yarn ends need to be sewn into the seams. One at a time, thread the yarn ends into a tapestry needle and weave them into the seam. Cut off the end of the yarn.

Abbreviations

Knitting patterns are usually written with abbreviations in order to save space. Below are listed all the abbreviations used in this book.

alt alternate

beg begin/beginning

CC contrast colour

cm centimetre(s)

cont continue

dec decrease (such as k2tog or p2tog)

DPN double-pointed needle

g gram(s)

in inch(es)

inc increase (such as kfb or pfb)

k knit

k2tog knit two (or specified number of) stitches together

kfb knit into the front and back of the same stitch to increase

m1 make one stitch

MC main colour

mm millimetre(s)

p purl

p2tog purl two (or specified number of) stitches together

p2togtbl purl two stitches together through the back loops

pfb purl into the front and back of the same stitch to increase

patt pattern

PB place bead: yarn forward, slip bead to front of work, slip 1 st purlwise, take yarn to back of work. Bead will now be sitting in front of slipped stitch

rem remaining

rep repeat

rev st st reverse stocking stitch

RS right side of work

skpo slip the first stitch, knit the second stitch, pass the slipped stitch over

sk2po slip the first stitch, knit the next two stitches together (as in k2tog), pass the slipped stitch over

sl slip

sppo slip the first stitch, purl the second stitch, pass the slipped stitch over

ssk slip the next two stitches one at a time knitwise, then knit them together through the front loops

st st stocking stitch

st/sts stitch/stitches

WS wrong side of work

yb yarn back

yfwd yarn forward

yo yarn over

* repeat instructions between * as many times as instructed

( ) repeat instructions between ( ) as many times as instructed (NB: square brackets are used for repeated instructions within repeated instructions)

Accessories

Accessories can be inspiring projects to tackle, as they are often small-scale, relatively quick to make and wearable! In this section we feature a range of projects, from beaded jewellery and quirky animal ears to a stylish Fair Isle tote and beret set.

Animal Ears

These ears are quick to make and fun to wear, and would be an entertaining addition to a fancy-dress costume. We offer three variations: bear cub, pussy cat and bunny rabbit.

Materials

For each set of ears you will need:
50g ball of DK (light worsted) yarn in main colour (MC)
50g ball of DK (light worsted) yarn in contrast colour (CC)
Thin plastic headband in similar colour to main yarn
Pair of 5mm (US: 8) double-pointed needles (DPNs)
Pair of 5mm (US: 8) straight needles
Toy stuffing
Safety pin
Tapestry needle

Sizes

Bear cub ears: 6.5 x 4cm (2½ x 1½in)
Pussy cat ears: 7 x 5.5cm (2¾ x 2¼in)
Bunny rabbit ears: 7 x 12cm (2¾ x 4¾in)

Tension (gauge)

18 sts and 25 rows over 10cm (4in) square in st st on 5mm (US: 8) needles.

Headband

Using DPNs and MC, make a 3-stitch i-cord (see page 23) the length of the headband, leaving long tails at either end. If you are using a wider headband, increase the number of stitches for the i-cord. Feed a thin plastic headband through the i-cord. You may find it easier to attach a safety pin at one end to help pull the cord around. Secure the covering in place using the long tails and weave in ends. Once your chosen animal ears are complete, pop them on your head and enjoy some creature comforts!

Front (make 2)

Using straight needles and MC, cast on 15 sts. You will now work with both the MC and CC using the intarsia technique (see page 24).

Row 1 (RS): K4MC, k7CC, k4MC.
Row 2 (WS): P4MC, p7CC, p4MC.
Row 3: K5MC, k5CC, k5MC.
Row 4: P5MC, p5CC, p5MC.
Row 5: K6MC, k3CC, k6MC.
Row 6: P1MC, sppoMC, p3MC, p3CC, p3MC, p2togMC, p1MC. (13 sts)
Break off CC and cont in MC only.
Row 7: K1, skpo, k7, k2tog, k1. (11 sts)
Row 8: P1, sppo, p5, p2tog, p1. (9 sts)
Row 9: K1, skpo, k3, k2tog, k1. (7 sts)
Row 10: Purl.
Cast off loosely knitwise.

Making up

Weave in ends.

Hold a back and a front piece together, WS facing each other.

Using MC, pick up and knit 8 sts along first side, 4 sts along top edge and 8 sts along second side, making sure to pick up sts through both pieces. (20 sts)
Cast off knitwise.

Lightly stuff as desired and repeat for second ear.

Bear cub ears
Back (make 2)

Using straight needles and MC, cast on 15 sts.

Starting with a knit row, work 5 rows in st st.
Row 6 (WS): P1, sppo, p9, p2tog, p1. (13 sts)
Row 7 (RS): K1, skpo, k7, k2tog, k1. (11 sts)
Row 8: P1, sppo, p5, p2tog, p1. (9 sts)
Row 9: K1, skpo, k3, k2tog, k1. (7 sts)
Row 10: Purl.
Cast off loosely knitwise.

Pin the ears in place on the headband (see page 32 for how to make the headband), checking the placement in a mirror or on an obliging friend. Stitch the ears to the headband, making sure that the bottom edge is also securely sewn together. Weave in ends.

Pussy cat ears

Back (make 2)

Using straight needles and MC, cast on 15 sts.

Starting with a knit row, work 6 rows in st st.

Row 7 (RS): K1, skpo, k9, k2tog, k1. (13 sts)

Row 8 (WS): Purl.

Row 9: K1, skpo, k7, k2tog, k1. (11 sts)

Row 10: P1, sppo, p5, p2tog, p1. (9 sts)

Row 11: K1, skpo, k3, k2tog, k1. (7 sts)

Row 12: P1, sppo, p1, p2tog, p1. (5 sts)

Row 13: K1, sk2po, k1. (3 sts)

Row 14: P3tog. (1 st)

Row 15: Knit.

Fasten off.

Front (make 2)

Using straight needles and MC, cast on 15 sts. You will now work with both the

MC and CC using the intarsia technique (see page 24).

Row 1 (RS): K4MC, k7CC, k4MC.

Row 2 (WS): P4MC, p7CC, p4MC.

Row 3: K4MC, k7CC, k4MC.

Row 4: P5MC, p5CC, p5MC.

Row 5: K5MC, k5CC, k5MC.

Row 6: As Row 4.

Row 7: K1MC, skpoMC, k3MC, k3CC, k3MC, k2togMC, k1MC. (13 sts)

Row 8: P5MC, p3CC, p5MC.

Row 9: K1MC, skpoMC, k3MC, k1CC, k3MC, k2togMC, k1MC. (11 sts)

Break off CC and cont in MC only.

Row 10: P1, skpo, p5, p2tog, p1. (9 sts)

Pin the ears in place on the headband (see page 32 for how to make the headband), checking the placement in a mirror or on an obliging friend. Stitch the ears to the headband, making sure that the bottom edge is also securely sewn together. Weave in ends.

Bunny rabbit ears

Back (make 2)

Using straight needles and MC, cast on 9 sts.

Row 1 (RS): Knit.
Row 2 (WS): P1, inc, p5, inc, p1. (11 sts)
Row 3: Knit.
Row 4: P1, inc, p7, inc, p1. (13 sts)
Row 5: Knit.
Row 6: Purl.
Row 7: K1, inc, k9, inc, k1. (15 sts)
Starting with a purl row, work 13 rows in st st.
Row 21: K1, skpo, k9, k2tog, k1. (13 sts)
Row 22: Purl.
Row 23: K1, skpo, k7, k2tog, k1. (11 sts)
Row 24: Purl.
Row 25: K1, skpo, k5, k2tog, k1. (9 sts)
Row 26: Purl.
Row 27: K1, skpo, k3, k2tog, k1. (7 sts)
Row 28: Purl.

Row 11: K1, skpo, k3, k2tog, k1. (7 sts)
Row 12: P1, sppo, p1, p2tog, p1. (5 sts)
Row 13: K1, skpo, k1. (3 sts)
Row 14: P3tog. (1 st)
Row 15: Knit.
Fasten off.

Making up

Weave in ends.
Hold a back and a front piece together, WS facing each other.
Using MC, sew the pieces together with blanket stitch.
Lightly stuff as desired and repeat for second ear.

Row 29: K1, skpo, k1, k2tog, k1. (5 sts)
Row 30: Purl.
Cast off loosely knitwise.

Front (make 2)

Using straight needles and MC, cast on
9 sts. You will now work with both the
MC and CC using the intarsia technique
(see page 24).
Row 1 (RS): Knit.
Row 2 (WS): P1, inc, p5, inc, p1. (11 sts)
Row 3: Knit.
Row 4: P1MC, incMC, p3MC, p1CC,
p3MC, incMC, p1MC. (13 sts)
Row 5: K5MC, k3CC, k5MC.
Row 6: P4MC, p5CC, p4MC.
Row 7: K1MC, incMC, k2MC, k5CC,
k2MC, incMC, k1MC. (15 sts)
Row 8: P4MC, p7CC, p4MC.
Row 9: K4MC, k7CC, k4MC.
Rep last 2 rows 5 more times.
Row 20: P5MC, p5CC, p5MC.
Row 21: K1MC, skpoMC, k2MC, k5CC,
k2MC, k2togMC, k1MC. (13 sts)
Row 22: P5MC, p3CC, p5MC.
Row 23: K1MC, skpoMC, k3MC, k1CC,
k3MC, k2togMC, k1MC. (11 sts)
Break off CC and cont in MC only.
Row 24: Purl.
Row 25: K1, skpo, k5, k2tog, k1. (9 sts)

Row 26: Purl.
Row 27: K1, skpo, k3, k2tog, k1. (7 sts)
Row 28: Purl.
Row 29: K1, skpo, k1, k2tog, k1. (5 sts)
Row 30: Purl.
Cast off loosely knitwise.

Making up

Weave in ends.
Hold a back and a front piece together,
WS facing each other.
Using MC, sew the pieces together with
backstitch.
Lightly stuff as desired and repeat for
second ear.
Fold over top of one ear (as shown in
pictures) and stitch in place.
Pin the ears in place on the headband
(see page 32 for how to make the
headband), checking the placement in a
mirror or on an obliging friend.
Stitch the ears to the headband, making
sure that the bottom edge is also
securely sewn together.
Weave in ends.

Beaded Jewellery

This dazzling necklace is knitted from wire using the i-cord method (see page 23). The beads provide a glittering effect, and long beaded tassels are used as a simple fastening. A bracelet made in a similar way is shown on page 41.

Necklace

Materials
One spool of 28-gauge craft wire
Small amount of 4ply (sport-weight) cotton yarn in turquoise
Pair of 3.25 mm (US: 3) double-pointed needles (DPNs)
Approx. 91 x 3mm turquoise beads to fit on wire

Size
1 x 31cm (⅜ x 12¼in) excluding ties

Tension (gauge)
Achieving a specific tension is not required for this project.

Special abbreviation
PB (place bead): Bring wire forward between needles, slip bead to front of work, slip 1 st purlwise, take wire to back of work. Bead will now be sitting in front of the slipped stitch.

The necklace is made using the i-cord technique (see page 23). Once you have cast on your stitches, knit one row. Do not turn. Instead, slide the stitches to the other end of the DPN, ready to be knitted again. The working end of the wire will now be at the left edge of the knitting; pull the wire tightly across the back of your work and then knit another

39

row. Continue in this way, never turning and always sliding the work to the other end of the DPN; the right side of the work will always be facing you.

Using the technique as described, make the necklace as follows:

Using wire, cast on 5 sts.
Row 1 (RS): Knit.
Rep last row 7 more times.
Row 9: K1, PB, k1, PB, k1.
Row 10: Knit.
Row 11: K2, PB, k2.
Row 12: Knit.
Rep last 4 rows until work measures 28cm (11in) from cast-on edge, ending with a Row 9.
Next row: Knit.
Rep last row 7 more times.
Cast off.

TIES

Cut two 35cm (14in) lengths of the cotton yarn. Fold one strand in half, then thread the folded loop through the centre of the cast-on edge of the wire i-cord, fold the ends of yarn back through the loop and pull to secure. Do the same with the second strand at the centre of the cast-off edge of the wire i-cord. Thread five beads onto the each end of both strands of cotton yarn, then secure with a knot.

Bracelet

Materials
One spool of 28-gauge craft wire
Pair of 3.25mm (US: 3) double-pointed needles (DPNs)
Approx. 72 x 3mm green beads to fit on wire
Clasp

Size
5mm x 40cm (¼ x 16in) excluding clasp

Special abbreviation
PB (place bead): Bring wire forward between needles, slip bead to front of work, slip 1 st purlwise, take wire to back of work. Bead will now be sitting in front of the slipped stitch.

The bracelet is also made using the i-cord technique. Following the instructions on page 23, make the bracelet as follows:

Using wire, cast on 3 sts.
Row 1 (RS): Knit.
Row 2 (RS): K1, PB, k1.
Rep last 2 rows until work measures
40cm (16in) from cast-on edge.
Next row: Knit.
Cast off.

Making up
Attach the clasp to the ends of the
bracelet using wire. Wear the bracelet
twisted twice around the wrist.

Tweed Gloves

Accessories can be both fun and practical. Flirty frills accent the cuff of these stylish gloves, while tweedy wool yarn will keep your hands toasty all winter long.

Materials
50g ball of DK (light worsted) wool, alpaca and viscose blend tweed yarn in apple green (A)
25g ball of 4ply (sport-weight) kid mohair and silk blend yarn in lime green (used double) (B)
50g ball of DK (light worsted) cotton yarn in gooseberry green (C)
Pair of 3.25mm (US: 3) needles
Pair of 4mm (US: 6) needles
Tapestry needle

Size
To fit average-size adult woman's hand

Tension (gauge)
22 sts and 30 rows over 10cm (4in) square in st st on 4mm (US: 6) needles.

Right hand
Using 3.25mm needles and yarn B, cast on 173 sts. Change to yarn C.
Row 1 (RS): K1, (k2, lift first of these sts over second and off needle) to end. (87 sts)
Row 2 (WS): P1, (p2tog) to end. (44 sts)
Change to yarn A.
Row 3: (K1, p1) to end.
Rep last row 23 more times, ending with a WS row.
Change to 4mm needles.
Next row: K7, m1, knit to last 7 sts, m1, k7. (46 sts)
Next row: Purl.
Next row: Knit.
Next row: Purl.

*SHAPE THUMB
Next row: K23, m1, k3, m1, knit to end. (48 sts)
Next row: Purl.
Next row: K23, m1, k5, m1, knit to end. (50 sts)

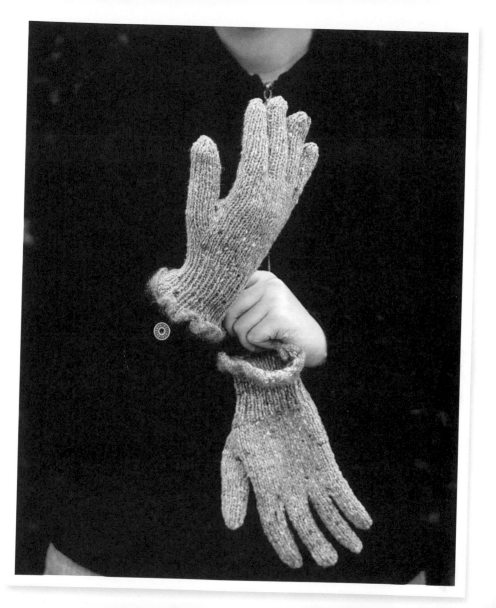

Next row: Purl.
Next row: K23, m1, k7, m1, knit to end. (52 sts)
Next row: Purl.
Next row: K23, m1, k9, m1, knit to end. (54 sts)
Next row: Purl.
Next row: K23, m1, k11, m1, knit to end. (56 sts)
Next row: Purl.
Next row: K23, m1, k13, m1, knit to end. (58 sts)
Next row: Purl.

DIVIDE FOR THUMB

Next row: K38, turn.
**Next row: P15, turn.
Starting with a knit row, work 14 rows in st st on these 15 sts only, ending with a WS row.
Next row: (K1, k2tog) to end. (10 sts)
Next row: Purl.
Next row: (K2tog) to end. (5 sts)
Break off yarn, thread through rem sts and pull tight.
With RS facing, rejoin yarn to rem sts at base of thumb and knit to end. (43 sts)
Next row: Purl.
Next row: Knit.
Next row: Purl.

Rep last 2 rows 4 more times, ending with a WS row.

FIRST FINGER

Next row: K28, turn.
Next row: P13, turn, cast on 2 sts. (15 sts)
Starting with a knit row, work 18 rows in st st on these 15 sts only, ending with a WS row.
Next row: (K1, k2tog) to end. (10 sts)
Next row: Purl.
Next row: (K2tog) to end. (5 sts)
Break off yarn, thread through rem sts and pull tight.

SECOND FINGER

With RS facing, rejoin yarn to rem sts, then pick up 2 sts from base of first finger and k5, turn.
Next row: P12, turn, cast on 2 sts. (14 sts)
Starting with a knit row, work 20 rows in st st on these 14 sts only, ending with a WS row.
Next row: (K1, k2tog) to last 2 sts, k2. (10 sts)
Next row: Purl.
Next row: (K2tog) to end. (5 sts)
Break off yarn, thread through rem sts and pull tight.

THIRD FINGER

With RS facing, rejoin yarn to rem sts, then pick up 2 sts from base of second finger and k5, turn.

Next row: P12, turn, cast on 2 sts. (14 sts)

Starting with a knit row, work 18 rows in st st on these 14 sts only, ending with a WS row.

Next row: (K1, k2tog) to last 2 sts, k2. (10 sts)

Next row: Purl.

Next row: (K2tog) to end. (5 sts)

Break off yarn, thread through rem sts and pull tight.

FOURTH FINGER

With RS facing, rejoin yarn to rem sts, then pick up 2 sts from base of third finger and k5, turn.

Next row: P12, turn.

Starting with a knit row, work 14 rows in st st, ending with a WS row.

Next row: (K1, k2tog) to end. (8 sts)

Next row: Purl.

Next row: (K2tog) to end. (4 sts)

Break off yarn, thread through rem sts and pull tight.

Left hand

Work as for Right Hand until *.

SHAPE THUMB

Next row: K20, m1, k3, m1, knit to end. (48 sts)

Next row: Purl.

Next row: K20, m1, k5, m1, knit to end. (50 sts)

Next row: Purl.

Next row: K20, m1, k7, m1, knit to end. (52 sts)

Next row: Purl.

Next row: K20, m1, k9, m1, knit to end. (54 sts)

Next row: Purl.

Next row: K20, m1, k11, m1, knit to end. (56 sts)

Next row: Purl.

Next row: K20, m1, k13, m1, knit to end. (58 sts)

Next row: Purl.

DIVIDE FOR THUMB

Next row: K35, turn.

Work as for Right Hand from ** to end.

Making up

Sew thumb, finger and side seams. Weave in ends.

Cable Legwarmers

These chunky cable legwarmers will keep you feeling really cosy on the very coldest days. They work up quickly, and are an ideal introduction to the cable technique (see page 22).

Materials
4 x 100g balls of super-chunky (super-bulky) merino wool yarn in aqua
Set of four 10mm (US: 15) double-pointed needles (DPNs)
Cable needle
Tapestry needle

Size
Women's size small, with thigh measuring approx. 38cm (15in). Stitches can be added between cable columns to increase the size.

Tension (gauge)
10 sts and 12 rows over 10cm (4in) square in cable pattern on 10mm (US: 15) needles.

Special abbreviation
C4b (cable 4 back): Slip next 2 sts onto cable needle and hold at back of work, k2 from left needle and then k2 from cable needle.

TIPS
- For a variation on the pattern, knit to directly under the knee and cast off for a shorter version, lessening the length of ribbing, or add another colour and make stripes.
- Do not cast off too tightly or the legwarmers might cut off your circulation.
- Do not cast off too loosely or the legwarmers might slide right down the leg.

Legwarmers (make 2)

Cast on 26 sts. Divide the sts evenly over three DPNs and join to work in the round.

Rounds 1–10: (K1, p1) to end.
Round 11: (K4, p1) to last 2 sts, p2tog.
Rounds 12–13: (K4, p1) to end.
Round 14: (C4b, p1) to end.
Rounds 15–19: As Round 12.
Rep Rounds 14–19 until Round 39 has been worked.

Round 40: (C4b, p1, kfb) to end. (30 sts)
Rounds 41–45: (K4, p2) to end.
Round 46: (C4b, p2) to end.
Rep Rounds 41-46 until Round 69 has been worked.
Round 70: (C4b, p2, kfb) to end. (35 sts)
Rounds 71–73: (K4, p3) to end.
Round 74: (K1, p1) to last 2 sts, p2tog.
Rounds 75–84: (K1, p1) to end.
Cast off loosely.
Weave in ends.

Fair Isle Set

Zesty, contemporary colours bring traditional Fair Isle right up to date and make this bag and beret modern classics.

Materials

These yarn quantities will make both the tote and the beret:

50g balls of DK (light worsted) wool yarn:

4 x beige (A)
2 x olive green (B)
2 x fresh green (C)
2 x pale grey (D)
2 x plum (E)
2 x red (F)
2 x dark green (G)
Pair of 3.25mm (US: 3) needles
Pair of 4mm (US: 6) needles
Tapestry needle

Materials for lining the bag (optional)

Piece of fabric approx. 65 x 37cm (25½ x 14½in)
Sewing needle and thread

Size

Bag panels: 30 x 36cm (12 x 14in)
Hat: to fit standard adult head

Tension (gauge)

24 sts and 32 rows over 10cm (4in) square in st st on 4mm (US: 6) needles.

Fair Isle tote

Side panels (make 2)

Using 4mm needles and yarn A, cast on 73 sts.

Starting with a knit row, repeating the 8-st patt rep 9 times across each row and working edge st as indicated, work in st st from chart on page 51 as follows:
Work all 30 rows of chart 3 times, then chart rows 1–4 again, inc 1 st at centre

of last row and ending with a WS row.
(74 sts)

Break off contrast yarns and cont in yarn A only.

Change to 3.25mm needles.

Next row (RS): K2, (p2, k2) to end.

Next row: P2, (k2, p2) to end.

These 2 rows form rib.

Cont in rib for 6 more rows, ending with a WS row.

Next row: Rib 12, cast off 2 sts (to form eyelet hole for strap), rib to last 14 sts, cast off 2 sts (to form other eyelet hole for strap), rib to end.

Next row: Rib to end, casting on 2 sts over those cast off on previous row.

Work in rib for 8 more rows, ending with a WS row.

Cast off in rib.

Straps (make 2)

Using 3.25mm needles and yarn A, cast on 6 sts.

Starting with a knit row, work in st st until strap measures 128cm (50½in), ending with a WS row.

Cast off.

Making up

Weave in ends, then block and press the pieces.

Join the side panels along cast-on and row-end edges.

Starting on RS of work, take one end of one strap through one eyelet hole on one side panel, then take the other end of the same strap through the other eyelet hole on the same side panel. Join ends of strap. Thread ends of other strap through eyelet holes on other side panel and join ends in same way. (Straps will roll in on themselves to form soft tubes.)

If you are lining the bag, cut two pieces the same size as side panels, adding seam allowance along all edges except the top edge. Sew the two lining pieces together along the side and lower edges, leaving the upper (opening) edge open.

Slip the lining inside the bag, turn under the raw edge around the upper edge so that it lies just below the ribbed top of the knitted bag and sew neatly in place.

Fair Isle chart (for both tote and beret)

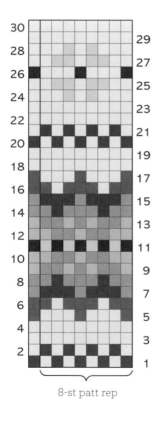

8-st patt rep

TIPS

- Lining the tote bag is a good idea as otherwise the floats or strands of yarn on the wrong side may become tangled with the contents of the bag and cause snags.
- You may want to block the beret over something circular such as a small plate to keep its shape.

KEY

- ☐ Yarn A
- ☐ Yarn B
- ☐ Yarn C
- ☐ Yarn D
- ■ Yarn E
- ■ Yarn F
- ■ Yarn G

Fair Isle beret

Beret

Using 3.25mm needles and yarn A, cast on 108 sts.

Row 1 (RS): (K1, p1) to end.

Row 2: As Row 1.

These 2 rows form rib.

Cont in rib for 7 more rows, ending with a RS row.

Row 10: Rib 1, m1, rib 1, (m1, rib 2) to end. (162 sts)

Change to 4mm needles.

Repeating the 8-st patt rep 20 times across each row and working first and last sts as indicated, work in st st from chart on page 51 as follows:

Work chart rows 1–18, ending with a WS row.

Row 19: With A, k1, (m1, k8) to last st, k1. (182 sts)

Row 20: (With E p1, with A p1) to end.

Row 21: (With E k1, with A k1) to end.

Row 22: With A, purl.

Row 23: With A, k1, (skpo, k7) to last st, k1. (162 sts)

Work chart rows 24–28.

Row 29: With A, k1, (skpo, k8) to last st, k1. (146 sts)

Row 30: With A, purl.

Repeating the 8-st patt rep 18 times across each row and working first and last sts as indicated, work in st st from chart as follows:

Work chart rows 1–2, ending with a WS row.

Row 33: With A, k1, (skpo, k7) to last st, k1. (130 sts)

Repeating the 8-st patt rep 16 times across each row and working first and last sts as indicated, work in st st from chart as follows:

Work chart rows 4–16, ending with a WS row.

Row 47: With A k1, with G k1, (with A skpo, k1, with G k1) to end. (98 sts)

Row 48: With A, purl.

Row 49: With A, k1, (skpo) to last st, k1. (50 sts)

Rows 50–51: As Rows 20–21.

Row 52: With A, p1, (p2togtbl) to last st, p1. (26 sts)

Row 53: As Row 49.

Break off yarn, thread through rem sts and pull tight.

Making up

Weave in ends, then block and press. Join back seam.

Babies and children

Knitting for babies and children is a lovely thing to do, whether for your own children or for those of friends and relatives. In this section we offer ideas for fun toys – finger puppets and a very cuddly elephant – as well as for clothes and accessories for babies and toddlers.

Baby Bootees

Here we offer three patterns for baby bootees to suit a range of tastes and styles.

Contrast-edge slippers
Materials

PINK AND GREEN VERSION
50g ball of DK (light worsted) mohair and lambswool blend yarn:
1 x pink (MC)
Small amount of green yarn (CC)

GREEN AND NAVY VERSION
50g ball of DK (light worsted) mohair and lambswool blend yarn:
1 x green (MC)
Small amount of navy yarn (CC)

Pair of 4mm (US: 6) needles
Tapestry needle

Size
To fit baby of 0–3 months

Tension (gauge)
22 sts and 40 rows over 10cm (4in) square in garter st on 4mm (US: 6) needles.

First slipper
SOLE
Using MC, cast on 14 sts and work in garter st.
Inc 1 st at each end of Rows 1, 3, 5 and 7. (22 sts)
Dec 1 st at each end of Rows 9, 11, 13 and 15. (14 sts)

UPPER
Row 16: Cast on 5 sts (for heel), k19.
Inc 1 st at beg of Rows 17, 19, 21 and 23 (for toe). (23 sts)
Row 24: Cast off 12 sts, knit to end.
Rows 25–35: Knit.
Row 36: Cast on 12 sts, k23.
Dec 1 st at beg of Rows 37, 39, 41 and 43. (19 sts)
Cast off.

TRIM
Using CC, pick up and knit 12 sts from heel to centre front, 6 sts across centre front and 12 sts from centre front to heel. Cast off.

Second slipper
Make second slipper to match.

Making up
Join heel seam. Carefully fit upper to sole, easing fullness around toe area, and stitch into position.
Weave in ends.

Textured shoes

Materials

50g ball of 4ply (sport-weight) cotton yarn in white
Pair of 2.75mm (US: 2) needles
Safety pin (for stitch holder)
2 small buttons

Size

To fit baby of 3–6 months

Tension (gauge)

28 sts and 38 rows over 10cm (4in) square in st st on 2.75mm (US: 2) needles.

First shoe

SOLE

Cast on 24 sts and work in moss st.
Inc 1 st at each end of Rows 2, 4, 6 and 8. (32 sts)
Dec 1 st at each end of Rows 12, 14, 16 and 18. (24 sts)
Row 19: Moss st to end, cast on 8 sts.

UPPER

Inc 1 st at beg of 2nd and every following alt row to 38 sts. (Row 12)

Row 13: Cast off 12 sts, moss 3, cast off 4 sts, moss st to end.
Row 14: Moss 19, leave 3 sts on safety pin.
Rows 15–25: Moss st.
Row 26: Moss 19, cast on 19 sts.
Row 27: Moss st.
Row 28: Dec 1 st, moss st to end.
Rep last 2 rows 5 more times.
Cast off.

STRAP
Place 3 sts from safety pin onto needle.
Row 1: (Inc) twice, k1.
Rows 2–15: Moss st.
Row 16: Moss 2, cast off 1 st, moss 2.
Row 17: Moss 2, yo, moss 2.
Rows 18–20: Moss st.
Cast off.

Second shoe
Make second shoe to match.

Making up
Join heel seam. Carefully fit upper to sole, easing fullness around toe area, and stitch into position. Moss stitch is reversible: take care to stitch up the second shoe as a mirror image of the first shoe, thereby obtaining a left and a right shoe. Weave in ends. Stitch on the buttons.

Anchor bootees

Materials
50g balls of 4ply (sport-weight) wool yarn:
1 x navy (MC)
1 x cream (CC)
Pair of 3mm (US: 2) needles

Size
To fit baby of 3–6 months

Tension (gauge)
28 sts and 38 rows over 10cm (4in) square in st st on 3mm (US: 2) needles.

First bootee
CUFF
Using CC, cast on 42 sts. Change to MC and work 6cm (2½in) in k1, p1 rib, dec 1 st at end of last row. (41 st) Change to st st. Work 4 rows.

DIVIDE FOR TOP OF FOOT
K28, turn, p15, turn.
On 15 sts, work 8 rows.
Rows 9–18: Place anchor motif, working from chart on page 61.
Work 4 more rows (toe). Break off yarn.
With RS facing, rejoin MC and pick up 11 sts along side of foot, 15 sts across toe,

11 sts along side of foot and 13 sts on needle. (63 sts)
Cont as follows:
Row 1: Using MC, knit.
Rows 2–3: Using CC, knit.
Rows 4–5: Using MC, knit.
Rep last 4 rows twice more.
Break off CC and cont in MC only.

SHAPE SOLE
Row 1: K1, *k2tog, k25, k2tog*, k3, *to* again, k1.
Row 2: K26, k2tog, k3, k2tog, k26.
Row 3: K1, *k2tog, k22, k2tog*, k3, *to* again, k1.
Row 4: K23, k2tog, k3, k2tog, k23.
Row 5: K1, *k2tog, k19, k2tog*, k3, *to* again, k1.
Cast off.

Second bootee
Make second bootee to match.

Making up
Join leg and under-foot seams.
Weave in ends.

18

10
9

■ MC   ☐ CC

61

Finger Puppets

These finger puppets will encourage imaginative play and give hours of pleasure. Once you've mastered the simple pattern for the basic body, and have tried the octopus and mouse, delight and amuse your children by devising your own creatures to add to the cast.

Materials

Oddments of 4ply (sport-weight) cotton yarn in sky blue (A), mid-blue (B) and cream (C)
Oddments of yarn for embroidering faces and whiskers
Pair of 3mm (US: 2) needles
Toy stuffing
Tapestry needle

Tension (gauge)

23 sts and 32 rows over 10cm (4in) square in st st on 3mm (US: 2) needles.

Basic body

Cast on 15 sts.
Knit 2 rows.
Starting with a knit row, cont in st st until work measures 6cm (2½in) from cast-on edge, ending with a WS row.*
Shape top as follows:
Next row: (K1, k2tog) to end. (10 sts)
Next row: Purl.

Next row: (K2tog) to end. (5 sts)
Break off yarn, thread through rem sts, pull tight and sew seam.

Octopus

Body and head

Using yarn A, follow instructions for the basic body to *.
Shape head as follows:
Next row: K1, (m1, k1) to end. (29 sts)
Work 11 rows in moss st.
Next row: K1, (k2tog) to end. (15 sts)
Next row: Purl.
Next row: K1, (k2tog) to end. (8 sts)
Break off yarn, thread through rem sts and pull tight.

Legs (make 8)

Using yarn B, cast on 5 sts.
Work in st st for 7cm (2¾in).
Cast off.

Pull the work slightly – this allows it to coil into a roll.

Making up
Weave in ends. Join main seam on head and body piece, then stuff head section. With running stitch, sew around bottom of head and then draw up and secure (enclosing stuffing). Attach legs evenly around the body at the bottom of the head. Embroider the smiley face as illustrated.

Mouse

Body and head
Using yarn C, follow instructions for the basic body.

Tail
Using yarn C, cast on 5 sts.
Work in st st for 11cm (4¼in).
Next row: K2tog, k1, k2tog. (3 sts)
Next row: Purl.

Next row: K3tog and fasten off.
Pull the work slightly – this allows it to coil into a roll.

Ears (make 2)
Using yarn C, cast on 4 sts.
Work 2 rows in st st.
Next row: Cont in st st, inc 1 st at each end of this and every following alt row until there are 14 sts.
Work 3 more rows without shaping.
Next row: Dec 1 st at each end of this and every following row until there are 2 sts.
Next row: K2tog and fasten off.

Making up
Weave in ends. Attach the tail and ears. Embroider the face and whiskers as illustrated.

Loulou the Elephant

Share all your secrets with Loulou, a gentle woolly giant, who will never forget them. This sturdy creature is a delight to knit.

Materials

4 x 50g balls of DK (light worsted) wool tweed yarn in grey (A)
Small amount of 4ply (sport-weight) cotton yarn in white (B)
Pair of 3mm (US: 2) needles
Pair of 4mm (US: 6) needles
Toy stuffing
Tapestry needle

Tension (gauge)

22 sts and 30 rows over 10cm (4in) square using yarn A in st st on 4mm (US: 6) needles.

Note

Use 4mm needles and yarn A for all parts of elephant except for the tusks.

Head – side sections (make 2)

Cast on 25 sts. Knit 1 row.
Cont in st st throughout.
Inc 1 st at each end of next 2 rows. (29 sts)
Work 11 more rows without shaping.

Next row: Inc 1 st at each end of row. (31 sts)
Work 12 more rows without shaping.
Next row: Dec 1 st at each end of row. (29 sts)
Work 14 more rows without shaping.
Rep the dec row 5 more times. (19 sts)
Cast off.

Head – centre gusset, top

Cast on 7 sts.
Work 7 rows in st st.
Next row: Inc 1 st at each end of row. (9 sts)
Rep last 8 rows 7 more times. (23 sts)
Work 30 more rows without shaping.
Next row: Dec 1 st at each end of row. (21 sts)
Work 11 more rows without shaping.
Rep the dec row 8 more times. (5 sts)
Cast off.

Head – centre gusset, under trunk

Cast on 7 sts.
Work 11 rows in st st.

Next row: Inc 1 st at each end of row.
(9 sts)
Rep last 12 rows 5 more times. (19 sts)
Cast off.

Ears (make 2)

Cast on 17 sts. Knit 1 row.
Cont in garter st throughout.
Inc 1 st at each end of next 6 rows.
(29 sts)
Next row: Knit to last 2 sts, (inc) twice.
(31 sts)
Work 18 more rows without shaping.
Next row: (K2tog, k3) to last st, k1. (25 sts)
Next row: (K2tog) 3 times, k13, (k2tog)
3 times. (19 sts)
Cast off.

Body – front and back (both alike)

Cast on 20 sts.
Work in st st throughout.
Work 2 rows.
Next row: Inc 1 st at each end of this
and every following alt row until there
are 30 sts.
Next row: Inc 1 st at each end of this
and every following 4th row until there
are 40 sts.
Work 24 more rows without shaping.
Next row: Dec 1 st at each end of this

and every following 4th row until there
are 20 sts.
Next row: K2tog, knit to end. (19 sts)
Cast off.

Arms (make 2)

Cast on 25 sts.
Work 22 rows in st st.
Cast off.

Legs (make 2)

Cast on 30 sts.
Work 30 rows in st st.
Cast off.

Pads – for arms (make 2)

Cast on 6 sts.
Work 2 rows in st st.
Next row: Inc 1 st at each end of row.
(8 sts)
Next row: Purl.
Next row: Inc 1 st at each end of row.
(10 sts)
Work 5 more rows without shaping.
Next row: Dec 1 st at each end of this
and following alt row. (6 sts)
Cast off.

Pads – for legs (make 2)

Cast on 6 sts.

Work 2 rows in st st.
Next row: Inc 1 st at each end of this and following 2 alt rows. (12 sts)
Work 5 more rows without shaping.
Next row: Dec 1 st at each end of this and following 2 alt rows. (6 sts)
Cast off.

Tail
Cast on 7 sts.
Work 14 rows in st st.
Next row: Dec 1 st at each end of this and every following 4th row until there are 3 sts.
Work 3 more rows without shaping.
Break off yarn, thread through rem sts and pull tight.
Cut short lengths of yarn, knot together, place in the point of the tail and sew side seam using mattress stitch.

Tusks (make 2)
Using 3mm needles and yarn B, cast on 7 sts.
Work 30 rows in st st.
Next row: K1, k2tog, k1, k2tog, k1. (5 sts)
Next row: Purl.
Next row: K2tog, k1, k2tog. (3 sts)
Next row: Purl.
Next row: K3tog and fasten off.

Making up
Weave in ends. Join all pieces using mattress stitch. Attach sides of head to main gusset. Insert lower gusset and stuff, leaving neck edges open. Join the body sections and sew on the head. Sew the side seams of arms and legs and insert pads; stuff. Attach to body (make sure the elephant will sit on a flat surface). Sew on the tail. Join tusk seams and draw up to make the tusk curve slightly. Sew on under the trunk. Embroider the eyes in yarn B.

Lacy Shawl

A hand-knitted shawl makes a beautiful heirloom gift for a baby. Using a wool and cotton blend yarn makes the shawl both soft against the skin and practical, as it is easily laundered.

Materials

12 x 50g balls of DK (light worsted) wool and cotton blend yarn in soft white
Pair of 3.75mm (US: 5) needles (you may prefer to use a long circular needle to accommodate the large number of stitches)

Size

137cm (54in) square

Tension (gauge)

23 sts and 18 rows over 10cm (4in) square in garter st on 3.75mm (US: 5) needles.

Shawl

Cast on 341 sts.
Rows 1–28: Knit (garter st).
Row 29: K22, *m1, k2tog, k3, rep from * to last 24 sts, m1, k2tog, k22.
Row 30: K23, *m1, k2tog, k3, rep from * to last 23 sts, m1, k2tog, k21.
Rep last 2 rows 20 more times.
Row 71: K22, *m1, k2tog, k3*, rep from * to * 5 more times, m1, k2tog, knit to last 54 sts, rep from * to * 6 more times, m1, k2tog, k22.
Row 72: K23, *m1, k2tog, k3*, rep from * to * 5 more times, m1, k2tog, knit to last 53 sts, rep from * to * 6 more times, m1,

TIP

To narrow the width of the shawl, simply reduce the number of stitches you cast on, to make the central panel smaller.

k2tog, k21.
Rep last 2 rows 145 more times.
Rep Rows 29–30 a further 21 times.
Knit 28 rows (garter st).
Cast off.

Finishing

Weave in ends. Pin out the shawl to
measurement (see finished size) and
gently press on the wrong side using
a steam iron.

Toddler's Sweater

This charming sweater is designed in two colours: marine blue and natural grey. Marine blue is the main colour, used for the larger stripes and the ribbed bottom band, collar and cuffs. Two different shades of grey are used for the finer stripes.

Materials

50g balls of DK (light worsted) wool yarn:

8 x marine blue (A)

2 x pale grey (B)

2 x dark grey (C)

Pair of 3mm (US: 2) needles

Pair of 3.75mm (US:5) needles

Stitch holder

2 buttons

Size

To fit a four-year-old child

Chest measurement: 54cm (21¼in)

Tension (gauge)

10 sts and 10 rows over 4cm (1½in) square in garter st on 3.75mm (US: 5) needles.

Back

Using 3mm needles and yarn A, cast on 72 sts.

Row 1: Working into back of sts, (k1, p1) to end.

Row 2: (K1, p1) to end.

Rep last row until work measures 6cm (2½in) from cast-on edge.

Next row: Knit.

Change to 3.75mm needles and cont in garter st, working in stripes as follows:

*Using yarn A, knit 8 rows. Break off yarn.

Join yarn B, knit 6 rows. Break off yarn.

Rejoin yarn A, knit 12 rows. Do not break off yarn.

Join yarn C, knit 2 rows. Break off yarn.*

Rep from * to * twice more.

SHAPE ARMHOLES

Row 1: Using yarn A, cast off 4 sts, knit to end.

Row 2: Cast off 4 sts, knit to end.

Row 3: K2tog, knit to last 2 sts, k2tog.

Row 4: As Row 3.** (60 sts)

Maintaining correct stripe sequence, cont in garter st until you have worked five narrow yarn C stripes in total (from cast-on edge), finishing after a narrow yarn C stripe. Break off yarn.

SHAPE SHOULDERS

Row 1: Using yarn A, knit to last 6 sts, turn.

Row 2: Knit to last 6 sts, turn.

Rows 3–4: Knit to last 12 sts, turn.

Rows 5–6: Knit to last 18 sts, turn.

Row 7: Knit to end.

Cast off.

Front

Work as for Back until **. (60 sts)

Using yarn A, knit 4 rows. Break off yarn.

Join yarn B, knit 6 rows. Break off yarn.

DIVIDE FOR FRONT OPENING

Next row: Join yarn A, k30, slip rem 30 sts onto stitch holder, turn.

Working on first set of 30 sts for left half of front, knit 11 rows in A, 2 rows in C, 8 rows in A and 3 rows in B, finishing at front edge.

SHAPE NECK

Row 1: Still using yarn B, cast off 6 sts, knit to end.

Row 2: Knit.

Row 3: K2tog, knit to end. Break off yarn.

Join yarn A and rep last 2 rows 5 more times. (18 sts)

Join yarn C, knit 2 rows. Break off yarn.

SHAPE SHOULDER

Row 1: Using yarn A, knit.

Row 2: Knit to last 6 sts, turn.

Row 3: Knit to neck.

Row 4: Knit to last 12 sts, turn.

Row 5: Knit to neck.

Cast off knitwise.

Slip rem 30 sts from holder onto a 3.75mm needle, point to centre. Rejoin yarn A and work right half of front as follows:
Maintaining correct stripe sequence as for left half of front, knit 24 rows, finishing at front edge.

SHAPE NECK

Row 1: Using yarn B, cast off 6 sts, knit to end.
Row 2: Knit.
Row 3: K2tog, knit to end.
Row 4: Knit. Break off yarn.
Row 5: Join yarn A, k2tog, knit to end.
Row 6: Knit.
Row 7: K2tog, knit to end.
Row 8: Knit.
Rep last 2 rows 3 more times. (18 sts)
Using yarn A, knit 2 rows.
Join yarn B, knit 2 rows, finishing at neck edge.
Break off yarn.

SHAPE SHOULDER

Row 1: Using yarn A, knit to last 6 sts, turn.
Row 2: Knit to neck.
Row 3: Knit to last 12 sts, turn.

Row 4: Knit to neck.
Cast off purlwise.

Sleeves (make 2)

Using 3mm needles and yarn A, cast on 42 sts.
Row 1: Working into back of sts, (k1, p1) to end.
Row 2: (K1, p1) to end.
Rep last row 18 more times.
Row 21: (K5, k2tog) to end. (36 sts)
Change to 3.75mm needles and cont in garter st, following same stripe sequence as on Back, increasing by working into front and back of first st and last-but-one st on 9th row and every following 6th row until there are 64 sts on needle.
Maintaining correct stripe sequence, cont without further shaping until work measures 23cm (9in) from cast-on edge.

SHAPE TOP

Keeping stripes correct, cast off 4 sts at beg of next 2 rows.
Dec 1 st at each end of every following row until there are 16 sts.
Cast off.

Collar

Using 3mm needles and yarn A, cast on 86 sts.
Row 1: Working into back of sts, (k1, p1) to end.
Row 2: (K1, p1) to end.
Rep last row twice more.
Keeping continuity of rib, inc 1 st at each end of next row and every following alt row until there are 94 sts.
Cont in rib without further shaping for 10 rows.
Cast off in rib.

Making up

Weave in ends.
Omitting ribbing, press work on wrong side using a hot iron and damp cloth.
Join shoulders of back and front together.
Stitch sleeves into position.
Stitch side and sleeve seams.
Place cast-on edge of collar to neck edge and, starting and finishing 5mm (¼in) from front opening, stitch collar around neck.

Make two button loops on left side of front by twisting two strands of yarn together. Attach two buttons on right side of front to correspond.

Homewares

Knitting is a wonderful way of introducing colour and comfort into a home. This section offers a lovely variety of projects, from a colourful two-tone doorstop to a textured table runner and a quirky Japanese-style 'lucky cat' to welcome guests and bring good fortune.

Lucky Cat

Known as the *maneki-neko,* this traditional Japanese cat figure is not waving, but in fact beckoning. Pop this cheeky fellow in your window to greet passers-by and beckon in some good luck.

Materials

25g balls of 4ply (sport-weight) viscose and metallized fibre blend yarn:
2 x gold (A)
1 x red (B)
1 x green (C)
1 x black (D)
Set of five 3.25mm (US: 3) double-pointed needles (DPNs)
Pair of 3.25mm (US: 3) straight needles
Toy stuffing
Tapestry needle
Sewing needle
Black cotton thread
Pair of 6mm (¼in) black toy eyes
Gold bead

Size

Base: 9 x 7.5cm (3½x 3in)
Height from base to tip of ears:
approx. 17cm (6½in)
Circumference at widest point:
approx. 30cm (12in)

Tension (gauge)

Achieving a specific tension is not required for this project as long as a consistent tension is maintained for each section.

Note

The colourwork for the ears and the coin are worked using the Fair Isle method (see page 25). When working longer stretches of a single colour, twist the yarn at the back every four or five stitches to create a float. Try to keep the floats at an even tension or the finished fabric may be puckered.

Head and body

Worked from the top of the head down. Using DPNs and yarn A, cast on 8 sts. Divide the sts evenly over four DPNs and join to work in the round.
Round 1: Knit.
Round 2: Kfb of each st. (16 sts)

Round 3: Knit.

Round 4: ([K1, kfb] twice, k4) twice. (20 sts)

Round 5: ([K2, kfb] twice, [k1, kfb] twice) twice. (28 sts)

Round 6: Knit.

Stitch closed the centre hole at top of head.

Round 7: ([K3, kfb] twice, k6) twice. (32 sts)

Round 8: ([K4, kfb] twice, [k2, kfb] twice) twice. (40 sts)

Round 9: Knit.

Round 10: ([K5, kfb] twice, k8) twice. (44 sts)

Round 11: ([K6, kfb] twice, [k3, kfb] twice) twice. (52 sts)

Round 12: Knit.

Round 13: ([K7, kfb] twice, k10) twice. (56 sts)

Round 14: ([K8, kfb] twice, [k4, kfb] twice) twice. (64 sts)

Rounds 15–25: Knit.

Round 26: ([K8, k2tog] twice, k10) twice. (52 sts)

Round 27: Knit.

Round 28: ([K6, k2tog] twice, [k3, k2tog] twice) twice. (44 sts)

Round 29: Knit.

Round 30: ([K5, k2tog] twice, k8) twice. (40 sts)

Rounds 31–36: Knit.

Round 37: ([K5, kfb] twice, k8) twice. (44 sts)

Round 38: Knit.

Round 39: Knit.

Round 40: ([K6, kfb] twice, [k3, kfb] twice) twice. (52 sts)

Round 41: Knit.

Round 42: Knit.

Round 43: ([K7, kfb] twice, k10) twice. (56 sts)

Round 44: Knit.

Round 45: Knit.

Round 46: ([K8, kfb] twice, [k4, kfb] twice) twice. (64 sts)

Round 47: Knit.

Round 48: Knit.

Round 49: ([K9, kfb] twice, k12) twice. (68 sts)

Round 50: ([K10, kfb] twice, [k5, kfb] twice) twice. (76 sts)

Round 51: ([K11, kfb] twice, k14) twice. (80 sts)

Round 52: ([K12, kfb] twice, [k6, kfb] twice) twice. (88 sts)

Round 53: (K28, [k7, kfb] twice) twice. (92 sts)

Round 54: (K28, [k8, kfb] twice) twice. (96 sts)
Round 55: (K28, [k9, kfb] twice) twice. (100 sts)
Rounds 56–76: Knit.
Cast off knitwise.
Weave in ends.

Ears
BACK (MAKE 2)
Using straight needles and yarn A, cast on 15 sts.
Starting with a knit row (RS), work 4 rows in st st.
Row 5: K2tog, k11, k2tog. (13 sts)
Row 6: Purl.
Row 7: Knit.
Row 8: P2tog, p9, p2tog. (11 sts)
Row 9: Knit.
Row 10: P2tog, p7, p2tog. (9 sts)
Row 11: Knit.
Row 12: P2tog, p5, p2tog. (7 sts)
Row 13: K2tog, k3, k2tog. (5 sts)
Row 14: Purl.
Cast off knitwise.
Weave in ends.

FRONT (MAKE 2)
Using straight needles and yarn A, cast on 15 sts.
Row 1 (RS): Knit.
Row 2: P2A, join yarn B, p11D, p2A.
Row 3: K2A, k11B, k2A.
Row 4: P3A, p9B, p3A.
Row 5: K2togA, k1A, k9B, k1A, k2togA. (13 sts)
Row 6: P2A, p9B, p2A.
Row 7: K3A, k7B, k3A.
Row 8: P2togA, p1A, p7B, p1A, p2togA. (11 sts)
Row 9: K3A, k5B, k3A.
Row 10: P2togA, p1A, p5B, p1A, p2togA. (9 sts)
Row 11: K3A, k3B, k3A.
Row 12: P2togA, p1A, p3B, p1A, p2togA. (7 sts)
Break off yarn B and cont in yarn A only.
Row 13: K2tog, k3, k2tog. (5 sts)
Row 14: Purl.
Cast off knitwise.
Weave in ends.

Making up ears
Hold a front and a back piece together, WS facing each other. Using yarn A, oversew the edges together, leaving

the bottom open. Repeat for the second ear. Stuff both ears and then pin in place on top of head – you may find them easier to position if you stuff the head temporarily first. Stitch the ears in place using yarn A.

Face
Insert the black toy eyes.
Using yarn A, embroider the nose using a series of straight stitches. Embroider the mouth using yarn B and three straight stitches. (You may want to double your yarn for this to make the mouth stand out more.) Using black cotton thread (double stranded), embroider the shape of the eyes, plus some eyelashes and whiskers.

Base
Using straight needles and yarn B, cast on 30 sts.
Starting with a knit row (RS), work 40 rows in st st.
Cast off knitwise.
Weave in ends.
Stuff head and body.
Using yarn A, stitch base to bottom of body, positioning the cast-on edge of the base at the front of the body

(and the right side on the outside). This will form a rectangular base with the longest sides at the front and back. Weave in ends.

Bib
Using straight needles and yarn C, cast on 20 sts.
Starting with a knit row (RS), work 12 rows in st st.
Row 13: K2tog, k16, k2tog. (18 sts)
Row 14: Purl.
Row 15: Knit.
Row 16: P2tog, p14, p2tog. (16 sts)
Row 17: Knit.
Row 18: P2tog, p12, p2tog. (14 sts)
Row 19: K2tog, k10, k2tog. (12 sts)
Row 20: P2tog, p8, p2tog. (10 sts)
Cast off knitwise.
Weave in ends.
Using yarn C, stitch bib to front of cat.

Coin
The instructions for knitting the characters on the coin are written out below. If you prefer to work the colour changes from a chart, see the chart on page 85.
Using straight needles and yarn A, cast on 7 sts.

Chart for characters on coin

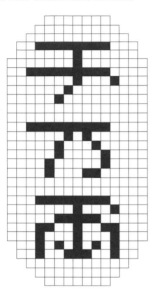

The characters on the coin translate as 'ten million ryo', the ryo being a now-antiquated form of currency in Japan. Ten million ryo would have been an enormous sum of money.

Row 1 (RS): Knit.
Row 2: Inc, p5, inc. (9 sts)
Row 3: Inc, k7, inc. (11 sts)
Row 4: Inc, join yarn D, p1D, p2A, p3D, p2A, p1D, incA. (13 sts)
Row 5: K2A, k1D, k1A, k1D, k1A, k1D, k1A, k1D, k1A, k1D, k2A.
Row 6: IncA, p1A, p1D, p3A, p1D, p3A, p1D, p1A, incA. (15 sts)
Row 7: K3A, k2D, k2A, k1D, k2A, k2D, k3A.
Row 8: P5A, p5D, p5A.
Row 9: K3A, k1D, k3A, k1D, k7A.
Row 10: P3A, p8D, p4A.
Row 11: Knit in A.
Row 12: Purl in A.
Row 13: K5A, k2D, k3A, k1D, k4A.
Row 14: P4A, p1D, p5A, p1D, p4A.
Row 15: K4A, k1D, k4A, k1D, k5A.
Row 16: P5A, p1D, p3A, p1D, p5A.
Row 17: K6A, k1D, k1A, k1D, k6A.
Row 18: P2A, p9D, p4A.
Row 19: Knit in A.
Row 20: Purl in A.
Row 21: K9A, k1D, k5A.
Row 22: P6A, p1D, p8A.
Row 23: K3A, k1D, k3A, k1D, k7A.
Row 24: P2A, p9D, p4A.
Row 25: K7A, k1D, k7A.

Row 26: P2togA, p5A, p1D, p5A, p2togA. (13 sts)
Row 27: K3A, k8D, k2A.
Break off yarn D and cont in yarn A only.
Row 28: P2tog, p9, p2tog. (11 sts)
Row 29: K2tog, k7, k2tog. (9 sts)
Row 30: P2tog, p5, p2tog. (7 sts)
Cast off knitwise.
Weave in ends.
Pin the coin to the front of the cat at an angle, with the top leaning towards the right arm. Stitch the coin in place using yarn A.
Using yarn B, embroider some toe lines for the back paws on the front of the cat, either side of the bottom of the coin.

Right arm
Using straight needles and yarn A, cast on 10 sts.
Starting with a knit row (RS), work 60 rows in st st.
Cast off knitwise.
Weave in ends.
Fold the arm in half along the short side, with RS facing each other. Using yarn A, stitch both sides together, leaving the bottom open. Turn the arm right side out and stuff.

Using yarn B, embroider some toe lines at the end of the arm for the paw. Pin the arm to the right side of body and stitch in place with yarn A.

Left arm

BACK

Using straight needles and yarn A, cast on 12 sts.

Starting with a knit row (RS), work 10 rows in st st.

Row 11: Cast off 5 sts, knit to end. (7 sts)
Starting with a purl row, work 8 rows in st st.

Row 20: Inc, p5, inc. (9 sts)
Starting with a knit row, work 4 rows in st st.

Row 25: K2tog, k5, k2tog. (7 sts)
Cast off purlwise.
Weave in ends.

FRONT

Using straight needles and yarn A, cast on 12 sts.

Starting with a purl row (WS), work 10 rows in st st.

Row 11: Cast off 5 sts, purl to end. (7 sts)
Starting with a knit row, work 9 rows in st st.

Row 20: Inc, k5, inc. (9 sts)
Starting with a purl row, work 4 rows in st st.

Row 25: P2tog, p5, p2tog. (7 sts)
Cast off knitwise.
Weave in ends.

Using yarn B, embroider some toe lines at the end of the front arm for the paw. Hold the front and back pieces together, with RS facing each other. Stitch the edges together with yarn A, leaving the base open. Turn right side out and stuff. Pin the arm to the left side of the body and stitch in place with yarn A.

Collar

Using two DPNs and yarn B, make a 4-stitch i-cord (see page 23) that is long enough to fit around the cat's neck. Cast off.

Stitch the collar in place with a few small stitches and join at the back of the neck. Sew a gold bead to the front centre of the collar to finish.

Hot Water Bottle Cover

This cosy accessory is made in a palette of warm colours; reverse stocking stitch is used to soften the changes between the stripes. The back of the design is asymmetrical, with the plain button flap contrasting with the stripe panel.

Materials

50g balls of DK (light worsted) yarn:
1 x coral (A)
1 x red (B)
1 x yellow (C)
1 x gold (D)
Pair of 4mm (US: 6) needles
Pair of 3.75mm (US: 5) needles
Two stitch holders
Tapestry needle
Three 18mm (¾in) buttons

Size

Width: 23cm (9in)
Length to neck: 27cm (10½in)

Tension (gauge)

22 sts and 30 rows over 10cm (4in) square in rev st st on 4mm (US: 6) needles.

Front

Using 4mm needles and yarn A, cast on 37 sts.
Row 1 (RS): Purl.
Row 2: Knit.
Row 3: Inc, purl to last st, inc. (39 sts)
Row 4: Inc, knit to last st, inc. (41 sts)
Rep last 2 rows once more. (45 sts)
Change to yarn B.
Row 7: Inc, purl to last st, inc. (47 sts)
Row 8: Inc, knit to last st, inc. (49 sts)
Change to yarn C.
Row 9: Inc, purl to last st, inc. (51 sts)
Change to yarn D.
Row 10: Inc, knit to last st, inc. (53 sts)

Row 11: Purl.
Row 12: Knit.
Change to yarn B.
Row 13: Purl.
Change to yarn C.
Row 14: Knit.
Rows 1–14 set the stripe pattern.
Rep Rows 1–14 (without shaping)
4 more times, ending with a WS row.
Cont in yarn A only.
Row 71: P2tog, purl to last 2 sts, p2tog.
(51 sts)
Row 72: K2tog, knit to last 2 sts, k2tog.
(49 sts)
Row 73: P2tog, purl to last 2 sts, p2tog.
(47 sts)
Row 74: K2tog, knit to last 2 sts, k2tog.
(45 sts)
Row 75: P2tog, purl to last 2 sts, p2tog.
(43 sts)
Row 76: Knit.
Row 77: Cast off 3 sts, purl to end. (40 sts)
Row 78: Cast off 3 sts, knit to end. (37 sts)
Rep last 2 rows once more. (31 sts)
Row 81: Cast off 4 sts, purl to end. (27 sts)
Row 82: Cast off 4 sts, knit to end. (23 sts)
Leave these 23 sts on a stitch holder.

Lower back

Using 4mm needles and yarn A, cast
on 37 sts.

Row 1 (RS): Purl.
Row 2: Knit.
Row 3: Inc, purl to last st, inc. (39 sts)
Row 4: Inc, knit to last st, inc. (41 sts)
Rep last 2 rows once more. (45 sts)
Change to yarn B.
Row 7: Inc, purl to last st, inc. (47 sts)
Row 8: Inc, knit to last st, inc. (49 sts)
Change to yarn C.
Row 9: Inc, purl to last st, inc. (51 sts)
Change to yarn D.
Row 10: Inc, knit to last st, inc. (53 sts)
Row 11: Purl.
Row 12: Knit.
Change to yarn B.
Row 13: Purl.
Change to yarn C.
Row 14: Knit.
Rows 1–14 set the stripe pattern.
Rep Rows 1–14 (without shaping) twice
more and then Rows 1–6 once again,
ending with a WS row.
Change to 3.75mm needles and yarn B.
Row 49: Knit.
Row 50: P4, (k3, p3) to last 7 sts, k3, p4.
Row 51: K4, (p3, k3) to last 7 sts, p3, k4.
Rep last 2 rows twice more.
Row 56: P4, (k3, p3) to last 7 sts, k3, p4.
Cast off in rib.

Upper back

Using 3.75mm needles and yarn B, cast on 53 sts.

Row 1 (RS): K4, (p3, k3) to last 7 sts, p3, k4.

Row 2: P4, (k3, p3) to last 7 sts, k3, p4. These 2 rows set the rib pattern.

Row 3: Rib 7, (k2tog, yfwd, rib 16) twice, k2tog, yfwd, rib 8.

Row 4: P4, (k3, p3) to last 7 sts, k3, p4.

Row 5: K4, (p3, k3) to last 7 sts, p3, k4.

Row 6: P4, (k3, p3) to last 7 sts, k3, p4. Change to 4mm needles and yarn A.

Row 7: Knit.

Row 8: Knit.

Row 9: Purl.

Rep last 2 rows 6 more times.

Row 22: Knit.

Row 23: P2tog, purl to last 2 sts, p2tog. (51 sts)

Row 24: K2tog, knit to last 2 sts, k2tog. (49 sts)

Rep last 2 rows once more.

Row 27: P2tog, purl to last 2 sts, p2tog. (43 sts)

Row 28: Knit.

Row 29: Cast off 3 sts, purl to end. (40 sts)

Row 30: Cast off 3 sts, knit to end. (37 sts)

Rep last 2 rows once more. (31 sts)

Row 33: Cast off 4 sts, purl to end. (27 sts)

Row 34: Cast off 4 sts, knit to end. (23 sts) Leave these 23 sts on a stitch holder.

Making up

Weave in ends. Sew front to upper back by sewing together the left-hand sets of cast-off stitches.

NECK OF COVER

With RS facing and using 3.75mm needles and yarn B, k22 from front stitch holder and then knit last st tog with first st from upper back stitch holder, knit to end. (45 sts)

Row 1 (WS): P3, (k3, p3) to end.

Row 2 (RS): K3, (p3, k3) to end.

Rep last 2 rows until neck measures 7.5cm (3in), ending with a RS row. Change to yarn A.

Next row: P3, (k3, p3) to end. Cast off loosely in rib.

Line up lower back with upper back, ensuring that the ribs overlap, and sew around all edges, leaving row ends of rib on upper back open. Position the three buttons along the rib of the lower back so that they line up with the buttonholes and sew in place.

Doorstop

This practical doorstop is a great way to bring some colour into a room. This two-colour project brings together a cool red-violet and a warm lime to create a dramatic palette.

Materials

50g balls of DK (light worsted) yarn:
2 x pink (A)
2 x green (B)
Pair of 4mm (US: 6) straight needles
60cm-long 4mm circular needle
(US: 24in-long size 6)
Pair of 4mm (US: 6) double-pointed
needles (DPNs)
Toy stuffing
Tapestry needle
Dried peas or rice to weight the doorstop
Four 2cm (¾in) buttons

Size

19cm (7½in) cube

Tension (gauge)

22 sts and 30 rows over 10cm (4in)
square in st st on 4mm (US: 6) needles.

Sides A and C (both alike)

Using straight needles and yarn A, cast on 41 sts.
Using the intarsia technique (see page 24) and changing colours as indicated, work all 53 rows of Chart 1 on page 96.
Using yarn A, purl 1 row.
Cast off.

Sides B and D (both alike)

Using straight needles and yarn B, cast on 41 sts.
Using the intarsia technique and changing colours as indicated, work all 53 rows of Chart 2 on page 96.
Using yarn B, purl 1 row.
Cast off.

Joining the sides

Sew the four sides (A–D) into a strip following diagram on page 97.

Top

With RS facing and using circular needle and yarn A, pick up and knit 162 sts across the top edge of the four side squares: 41 sts across top of first square, 40 sts across top of second, 40 sts across top of third and 41 sts across top of fourth.

Row 1 (WS): Knit.

Change to yarn B.

Row 2 (RS): K1, k2tog, k36, (ssk, k2tog, k36) to last 3 sts, ssk, k1. (154 sts)

Row 3: Purl.

Row 4: K1, k2tog, k34, (ssk, k2tog, k34) to last 3 sts, ssk, k1. (146 sts)

Row 5: Purl.

Row 6: K1, k2tog, k32, (ssk, k2tog, k32) to last 3 sts, ssk, k1. (138 sts)

Row 7: Purl.

Row 8: K1, k2tog, k30, (ssk, k2tog, k30) to last 3 sts, ssk, k1. (130 sts)

Row 9: Purl.

Row 10: K1, k2tog, k28, (ssk, k2tog, k28) to last 3 sts, ssk, k1. (122 sts)

Row 11: Purl.

Row 12: K1, k2tog, k26, (ssk, k2tog, k26) to last 3 sts, ssk, k1. (114 sts)

Row 13: Purl.

Row 14: K1, k2tog, k24, (ssk, k2tog, k24) to last 3 sts, ssk, k1. (106 sts)

Row 15: Purl.

Row 16: K1, k2tog, k22, (ssk, k2tog, k22) to last 3 sts, ssk, k1. (98 sts)

Row 17: Purl.

Row 18: K1, k2tog, k20, (ssk, k2tog, k20) to last 3 sts, ssk, k1. (90 sts)

Row 19: P1, p2togtbl, p18, (p2tog, p2togtbl, p18) to last 3 sts, p2tog, p1. (82 sts)

Working decreases as set by last 2 rows, continue decreasing on every row until there are 18 sts, ending with a WS row. Break off yarn, thread through rem sts and pull tight.

Base

Using straight needles and yarn A, cast on 41 sts.

Starting with a knit row (RS), work in st st until 56 rows have been worked, ending with a WS row.

Cast off.

Handle

The handle is made using the i-cord technique (see page 23). Using DPNs and yarn A, cast on 5 sts and knit one row. Do not turn. Instead, slide the stitches to the other end of the DPN, ready to be knitted again. The working

Chart 1

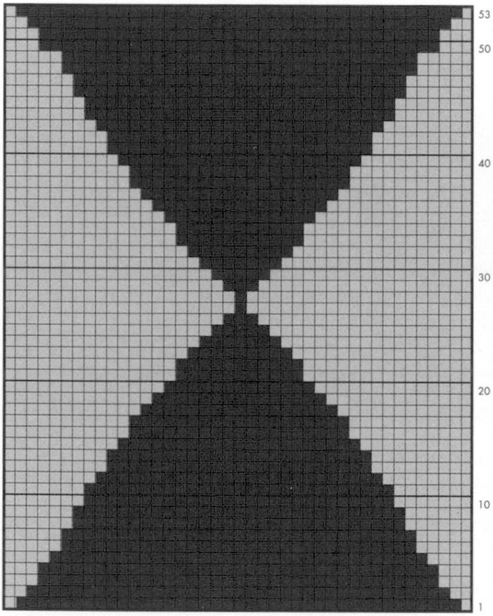

Chart 2

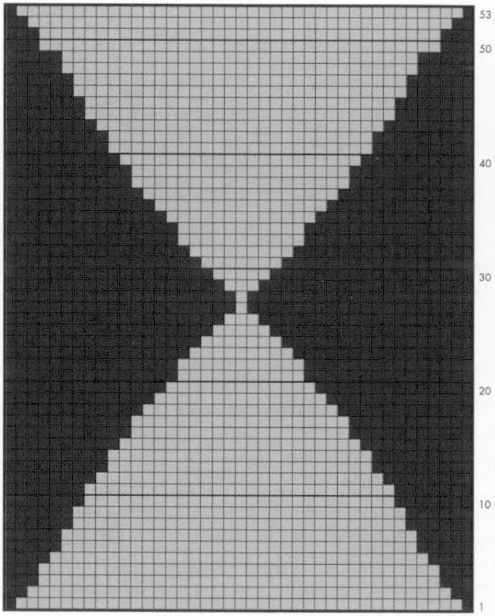

Diagram for joining the sides (see page 92)

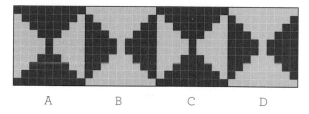

A   B   C   D

end of the yarn will be at the left edge of the knitting, so pull it tightly across the back of the work and then knit another row. Continue in this way, never turning and always sliding the work to the other end of the dpn so that the RS of the work is always facing you.

Cont until i-cord measures 15cm (6in) from cast on edge.

Break off yarn, thread through rem sts and pull tight.

Fold i-cord in half to form a loop and stitch the cast-on edge to the last row.

Making up

Weave in ends.

Starting at the bottom, sew the remaining side of square A to the remaining side of square D and sew all the way up to the end of the shaping at centre top.

With RS facing, sew the base to the bottom edges of each of the four side squares, leaving one seam open for inserting stuffing.

STUFFING

The doorstop is predominantly filled with toy stuffing, but to achieve the weight that it needs, try putting a layer of dried peas or rice at the bottom (in a fabric bag) and then insert the toy stuffing on top of this.

To achieve the studded effect, using the photograph as a guide sew each of the four buttons in place, lacing the thread from side to side through the centre of the doorstop.

Finally, stitch the loop handle in place at the centre top.

Table Runner

This table runner combines a range of neutral colours to produce a calm and well-balanced palette. This piece, showcasing a variety of textures, will be a pleasing feature on any dining table.

Materials

50g balls of DK (light worsted) yarn:
1 x chocolate brown (A)
5 x cream (B)
2 x beige (C)
Pair of 4mm (US: 6) needles
Cable needle
Tapestry needle

Size

26 x 137cm (10¼ x 54in)

Tension (gauge)

21 sts and 28 rows over 10cm (4in) square in moss st on 4mm (US: 6) needles.

Special abbreviations

C6b (cable 6 back): Slip next 3 sts onto cable needle and hold at back of work, k3 from left needle and then k3 from cable needle.

C6f (cable 6 front): Slip next 3 sts onto cable needle and hold at front of work, k3 from left needle and then k3 from cable needle.

First end section

Using yarn A, cast on 60 sts.
Change to yarn B.
Rows 1–2: Knit.
Change to yarn A.
Row 3 (RS): Knit.
Row 4: K3, purl to last 3 sts, k3.
Change to yarn C.
Rows 5–6: Knit.

Change to yarn A.

Row 7: K9, sl 2 sts, (k6, sl 2 sts) to last 9 sts, k9.

Row 8: K3, p6, sl 2 sts, (p6, sl 2 sts) to last 9 sts, p6, k3.

Change to yarn C.

Row 9: K9, sl 2 sts, (k6, sl 2 sts) to last 9 sts, k9.

Row 10: Knit.

Change to yarn A.

Row 11: Knit.

Row 12: K3, purl to last 3 sts, k3.

Change to yarn C.

Rows 13–14: Knit.

Change to yarn A.

Row 15: K5, sl 2 sts, (k6, sl 2 sts) to last 5 sts, k5.

Row 16: K3, p2, sl 2 sts, (p6, sl 2 sts) to last 5 sts, p2, k3.

Change to yarn C.

Row 17: K5, sl 2 sts, (k6, sl 2 sts) to last 5 sts, k5.

Row 18: Knit.

Change to yarn A.

Row 19: Knit.

Row 20: K3, purl to last 3 sts, k3.

Change to yarn C.

Rows 21–22: Knit.

Change to yarn A.

Row 23: K9, sl 2 sts, (k6, sl 2 sts) to last 9 sts, k9.

Row 24: K3, p6, sl 2 sts, (p6, sl 2 sts) to last 9 sts, p6, k3.

Change to yarn C.

Row 25: K9, sl 2 sts, (k6, sl 2 sts) to last 9 sts, k9.

Row 26: Knit.

Change to yarn A.

Row 27: Knit.

Row 28: K3, purl to last 3 sts, k3.

Change to yarn B.

Rows 29–30: Knit.

Change to yarn C.

Rows 31–32: Knit.

Centre section

Now work using the intarsia technique (see pages 24) as follows:

Row 33 (RS): Using yarn B p1, (k1, p1) 11 times, k1, p2, using yarn C k1, m1, (k2, m1) 3 times, k1, using yarn B p2, k1, (p1, k1) to last st, p1. (64 sts)

Row 34: Using yarn B p1, (k1, p1) 11 times, p1, k2, using yarn C k12, using yarn B k2, p1, (p1, k1) to last st, p1.

Row 35: Using yarn B p1, (k1, p1) 11 times, k1, p2, using yarn C k12, using yarn B p2, k1, (p1, k1) to last st, p1.

Row 36: As Row 34.

Row 37: Using yarn B p1, (k1, p1) 11 times, k1, p2, using yarn C c6b, c6f, using yarn B p2, k1, (p1, k1) to last st, p1.

Row 38: As Row 34.

Row 39: As Row 35.

Row 40: As Row 34.

Row 41: As Row 35.

Row 42: As Row 34.

Row 43: Using yarn B p1, (k1, p1) 11 times, k1, p2, using yarn C c6f, c6b, using yarn B p2, k1, (p1, k1) to last st, p1.

Row 44: As Row 34.

Row 45: As Row 35.

Row 46: As Row 34.

Rows 35–46 form the cable pattern. Rep these 12 rows until work measures 128cm (50½in) from cast-on edge, ending with a Row 45.

Next row: Using yarn B p1, (k1, p1) 11 times, p1, k2, using yarn C (p1, p2tog) 4 times, using yarn B k2, p2, (k1, p1) to end. (60 sts)

Second end section

Change to yarn C.

Next row (RS): Knit.

Next row: Knit.

Change to yarn B.

Next row: Knit.

Next row: Knit.

Change to yarn A.

Next row: Knit.

Next row: K3, purl to last 3 sts, k3.

Change to yarn C.

Next row: Knit.

Next row: Knit.

Change to yarn A.

Next row: K9, sl 2 sts, (k6, sl 2 sts) to last 9 sts, k9.

Next row: K3, p6, sl 2 sts, (p6, sl 2 sts) to last 9 sts, p6, k3.

Change to yarn C.

Next row: K9, sl 2 sts, (k6, sl 2 sts) to last 9 sts, k9.

Next row: Knit.

Change to yarn A.

Next row: Knit.
Next row: K3, purl to last 3 sts, k3.
Change to yarn C.
Next row: Knit.
Next row: Knit.
Change to yarn A.
Next row: K5, sl 2 sts, (k6, sl 2 sts) to last 5 sts, k5.
Next row: K3, p2, sl 2 sts, (p6, sl 2 sts) to last 5 sts, p2, k3.
Change to yarn C.
Next row: K5, sl 2 sts, (k6, sl 2 sts) to last 5 sts, k5.
Next row: Knit.
Change to yarn A.
Next row: Knit.
Next row: K3, purl to last 3 sts, k3.
Change to yarn C.
Next row: Knit.
Next row: Knit.
Change to yarn A.
Next row: K9, sl 2 sts, (k6, sl 2 sts) to last 9 sts, k9.

Next row: K3, p2, sl 2 sts, (p6, sl 2 sts) to last 5 sts, p2, k3.
Change to yarn C.
Next row: K9, sl 2 sts, (k6, sl 2 sts) to last 9 sts, k9.
Next row: Knit.
Change to yarn A.
Next row: Knit.
Next row: K3, purl to last 3 sts, k3.
Change to yarn B.
Next row: Knit.
Next row: Knit.
Change to yarn A.
Next row: Knit.
Cast off.

Finishing
Weave in ends.

Textured Cushion

A cushion is an ideal way of testing out your ideas for colour and stitchwork combinations. Here, three bands of Fair Isle framed by four moss stitch bands form the main panel of the cushion. This panel sits next to a simple stocking stitch panel, while a moss stitch button band separates the two.

Materials

50g balls of DK (light worsted) yarn:
2 x rich red (A)
1 x coral (B)
1 x tomato red (D)
1 x burgundy (E)
25g ball of 4ply (sport-weight) silk and mohair blend yarn in wine (used double) (C)
Pair of 4mm (US: 6) needles
Tapestry needle
Piece of fabric, approx. 43cm (17in) square, for back of cushion
Sewing machine
Sewing thread
Sewing needle
7 buttons of varying sizes, 15–20mm (½–¾in)
Cushion pad, 40cm (16in) square

Size

40cm (16in) square

Tension (gauge)

22 sts and 30 rows over 10cm (4in) square in pattern on 4mm (US: 6) needles.

Front Fair Isle panel

Using yarn A, cast on 61 sts.
Row 1 (RS): K1, (p1, k1) to end.
This row forms moss st.
Rep this row twice more.
Change to yarn C.
Rows 4–5: As Row 1.
Change to yarn A.
Rows 6–9: As Row 1.
Change to yarn C.
Rows 10–11: As Row 1.
Change to yarn A.
Rows 12–15: As Row 1.
Row 16: Purl.

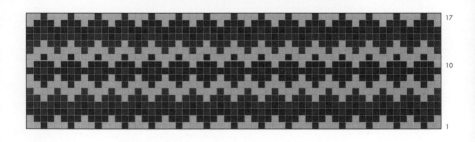

Starting with a knit row and working in st st, work all 17 rows of chart on page 106, changing colours as indicated.

Change to yarn A.

Row 34: Purl.

Rep Rows 1–34 twice more and then Rows 1–15 once again.

Next row: K1, (p1, k1) to end.

Cast off in pattern.

Front plain panel

Using yarn A, cast on 39 sts.

Starting with a knit row (RS), work in st st until plain panel measures same as Fair Isle panel from cast-on edge, ending with a WS row.

Cast off.

Button band

With RS of Fair Isle panel facing and using yarn E, pick up and knit 88 sts along right-hand edge of Fair Isle panel.

Row 1: (K1, p1) to end.

Row 2: (P1, k1) to end.

These 2 rows form moss st.

Rep these 2 rows twice more.

Row 7: Moss 4, cast off 2 sts, (moss 11 [includes st used to cast off], cast off 2 sts) to last 4 sts, moss st to end.

Row 8: Moss 4, turn, cast on 2 sts, turn, (moss 11, turn, cast on 2 sts, turn) to last 4 sts, moss st to end.

Row 9: (K1, p1) to end.

Row 10: (P1, k1) to end.

Row 11: (K1, p1) to end.

Cast off in pattern.

Making up

With RS facing, line up the left-hand edge of the plain panel with the pick-up edge of the button band on the Fair Isle panel so that the button band is lying on top of the plain panel. Use the position of the buttonholes to place the buttons correctly. Sew the buttons into place and then button them up to join the two panels.

Using the knitted cushion front as a template, cut backing fabric to size, allowing a 1.5cm (½in) seam allowance all the way around. Stitch the fabric to the cushion front. Insert the cushion pad through the button flap.

Textured Cushion Variations

Fair Isle patterns are a great way to explore colour variations. In the main version of this project (pages 104–107) we used different shades of red to stunning effect; here we try out some other colour combinations.

Gold and purple

This version exudes a sense of mellowness. Blending a DK-weight yarn with a slightly darker, fine mohair and using a simple slip stitch pattern helps achieve a subtle finish. The Fair Isle section is much bolder in this variation, picking up on the tones of fallen leaves and highlighting with purple. Balance is achieved by working the moss stitch button band in the ochre colour found in the Fair Isle section and by adding textured buttons in similar tones.

Materials

Yarn A = 2 balls of DK yarn
Yarn B = 1 ball of 4ply yarn
(used double)
Yarn C = 1 ball of DK yarn

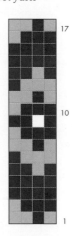

Finding inspiration

The main version of this cushion on pages 104–107 demonstrates attention to value, proportion and stitchwork, with these elements highlighted by the envelope structure and choice of buttons. Successfully changing the colour palette of the project involves keeping the various elements balanced, even if they all change completely. The mood boards on this page and on page 111 give you ideas on how to collect and arrange sources of inspiration to recolour the cushion.

The dried leaves and flowers of autumn provide a wealth of inspiration for colours. This mood board features a subtle blend of brown, gold and ochre along with the berry tone of damson.

Yarn D = 1 ball of DK yarn
Yarn E = 1 ball of DK yarn

Fair Isle section
See chart.

Stitchwork section
Worked over 61 sts as follows:
Change to yarn B.
Row 1: K2, yfwd, sl 1 st, yb, (k1, yfwd, sl 1 st, yb) to last 2 sts, k2.
Row 2: Purl.
Change to yarn A.
Row 3: K3, yfwd, sl 1 st, yb, (k1, yfwd, sl 1 st, yb) to last 3 sts, k3.
Row 4: Purl.
Rep last 4 rows 3 more times.

Button band
Worked in moss st in yarn E.

Grey, blue and lemon

The second variation moves from the mellow to the tranquil and uses a much cooler palette. The bands of garter stitch stripes echo the interplay of blues found in the inspiration piece (see page 111), while the Fair Isle section emphasizes how a different technique can impact on the way that we read colours. Focus is achieved with a dark blue garter stitch button band, while shell buttons reflect the association of blue with water.

Materials

Yarn A = 2 balls of DK yarn
Yarn B = 1 ball of DK yarn
Yarn C = 1 ball of DK yarn
Yarn D = 1 ball of DK yarn
Yarn E = 1 ball of DK yarn

Fair Isle section

See chart.

Stitchwork section

Worked over 61 sts as follows:

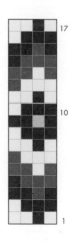

Mood board

You may find that you are inspired by a collection of fabrics for ideas on introducing colours and textures into your knitting. You will see from the mood board here that a piece of fabric (top right) set the feel for this reinterpretation of the cushion. Other inspiring objects such as stationery, buttons and pieces of ribbon were added to build up the range of colours. By highlighting certain colours in this way, the final colours of yarn can be selected based on the most effective and harmonious combinations. A soft yellow brings a pleasing contrast to the generally quite cool palette.

Change to yarn B.
Row 1: Knit.
Row 2: Knit.
Change to yarn A.
Row 3: Knit.
Row 4: Knit.
Change to yarn D.
Row 5: Knit.
Row 6: Knit.

Rep Rows 1–6 twice more and then Rows 1–2 once again.

Button band
Worked in garter stitch in yarn C.

Acknowledgements

Many thanks to the designers:
Animal ears and Lucky Cat by Vicky Eames; Beaded jewellery and Tweed gloves by Emma King; Cable legwarmers by Tanis Gray; Fair Isle set by Fiona McTague; Baby bootees by Zoe Mellor; Finger puppets and Loulou the Elephant by Tracy Chapman; Lacy shawl and Toddler's sweater by Judith More; Hot water bottle cover, Doorstop, Table runner and Textured cushion by Sarah Hazell and Emma King.

Many thanks to the photographers:
Sue Baker, Geoff Dann, Mario Guarino, Holly Jolliffe, Robin Lever, Rebecca Maynes, Michael Wicks and Christina Wilson.